sundance
LITTLE BLUE READERS

Baking a Cake

Focus: Designing, Making and Appraising

PETER SLOAN &
SHERYL SLOAN

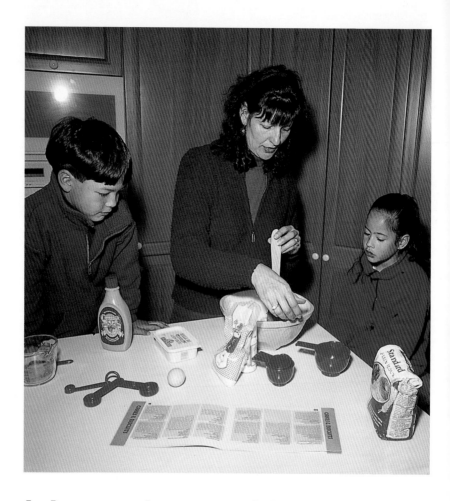

Mom is making a
chocolate cake.
Anna and Tony
will help her.

Anna mixes butter with sugar.
She mixes until all the lumps are gone.

Tony adds two eggs.
Some shell falls into
the bowl. Tony will
lift the shell out
with a spoon.

Anna adds flour and chocolate. Tony adds milk. He mixes everything together.

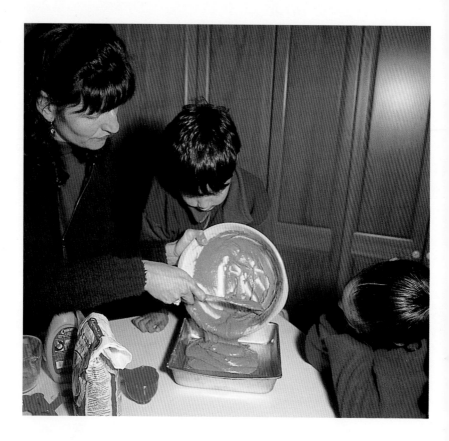

Mom spoons the wet cake mix into the pan. She puts the cake into the hot oven.

Anna, Tony, and
Mom clean up.
Anna and Tony lick
the spoon and the
bowl. They think this
is the best part.

Mom takes the cake
out of the oven.
When it cools, Anna
and Tony frost the
cake. Time to eat!